State of Vermont
Department of Libraries
Midstate Regional Library
RFD #4   Box 1870
Montpelier, VT 05602

Britain

Britain is a land of contrasts: climatically, geographically and socially. In parts of the country the summers are warm enough for palm trees to flourish; in others, the winters are harsh and bitter. In places it is empty and desolate, yet its cities are among the most overcrowded in the world. Britain is rich in resources and in enterprise, yet she currently faces one of the worst periods of depression and unemployment since the 1930s.

An island nation, Britain has at last been drawn closer to her neighbors in Europe through membership in the Common Market, thus ending hundreds of years of comparative economic and political isolation. Britain is a land rich in history and traditions which have been carefully preserved by its proud people.

In *We live in Britain*, a cross-section of these people tell you what their life is like – life in the countryside and in the towns; life on the farm and in the factory.

Chris Fairclough is a freelance photographer and author who has written numerous books for children.

we live in BRITAIN

Chris Fairclough

A Living Here Book

The Bookwright Press
New York · 1984

Living Here

We Live in Australia
We Live in Britain
We Live in China
We Live in Denmark
We Live in France
We Live in India
We Live in Israel
We Live in Italy
We Live in New Zealand
We Live in Spain

First published in the United States in 1984 by
The Bookwright Press, 387 Park Avenue South,
New York, NY 10016

First published in 1982 by
Wayland (Publishers) Ltd, England

© Copyright 1982 Wayland (Publishers) Ltd
All rights reserved

ISBN 0–531–04783–0

Library of Congress Catalog Card Number 83–72803

Printed by G. Canale & C.S.p.A. Turin, Italy

Contents

Harry Bowden, *coal miner* — 6
Tony Gregory, *dairy farmer* — 8
Brian Brown, *lifeboatman* — 10
Janet Lewis, *police constable* — 12
John Robertson, *distillery worker* — 14
Guftar Hussein, *shopkeeper* — 16
Arthur Robinson, *manager* — 18
Brede Arkless, *mountaineer* — 20
John Tribble, *publican (pub keeper)* — 22
Nigel Nice, *postman* — 24
Tony Quaife, *hovercraft captain* — 26
Josette Simon, *actress* — 28
Philip Duffy, *market gardener* — 30
Jean Duncan, *tourist guide* — 32
Pat Navin, *bus driver* — 34
Peter Hesketh, *teacher* — 36
Eveline Sabin, *hotel keeper* — 38
Don Morgan, *folksinger* — 40
Keith Best, *M.P. (Member of Parliament)* — 42
Fred Harding, *fisherman* — 44
Ray Anthony, *teenager* — 46
Gill Swain, *newspaper reporter* — 48
Andy Kay, *roughneck* — 50
Beryl James, *nurse* — 52
David Boorman, *cricket player* — 54
Dr. Michael Dewar, *rector* — 56
Jenny Smith, *student* — 58
Dayle Hunt, *automobile worker* — 60
Britain Facts — 62
Glossary — 63
Index — 64

"The best rugby team in the world"

Harry Bowden is 58 and lives in Abertridwr, a village near Caerphilly, South Wales. Harry is a miner at a colliery called Nantgawr about 8 km. (5 miles) from his home.

I went down the pit when I was 15. That was in the 1930s, and I was lucky to get a job at all. There was terrible unemployment here in the Welsh valleys during the depression.

The first coal mines in South Wales were sunk during the middle of the last century. They were all privately owned then. Life was hard for the men and boys who worked in them. Conditions have improved now of course. Most mines are nationalized and run by the National Coal Board (N.C.B.).

South Wales is known for the great variety of coal that it produces – anthracite, steam coal, house coal and coking coal. But it is a very difficult region to mine. There are hundreds of fault lines running deep across the valleys and this means that we have to remove a lot of rock to get to the coal. Some pits in Britain, especially those in Nottinghamshire and parts of Yorkshire have much larger reserves of coal and are easier to mine.

Altogether, there are 201 pits in Britain employing over 211,000 miners. We produce a total of about 120 million tons of coal a year. But here in South Wales, many of the mines are closing. It was a sad day for me when my own local pit, the Winsor colliery, closed in 1974. That was when I moved over the hill to

Like most of the 201 collieries in Britain, Nantgawr is nationalized and run by the National Coal Board.

A colorful girls' jazz band at the annual miners' gala in Cardiff, South Wales.

Nantgawr. There are 650 men employed here and we remove about 4,000 tons of coal a week. Most of it goes straight to the coking plant next door and then on to the Midlands car industry after processing. The remainder is used by the Central Electricity Generating Board in their power stations.

The mines are worked twenty-four hours a day in three, eight-hour, shifts. We go down the mineshaft in a lift (elevator) called a cage. We work about seven hours underground but it often takes us a long time just to get to the coal-face. Sometimes we walk, but often we catch an underground train. There are 24 km (15 miles) of roadways down Nantgawr colliery and 5 km (3 miles) of coal-carrying conveyor belts. The mines are a dangerous place to work and even after forty-four years in the job I'm still relieved to see the daylight again at the end of a shift.

Because so many miners travel to other valleys to work, the sense of belonging to a community that we used to have in South Wales is now disappearing fast. Some of the famous Welsh choirs are disbanding; people have given up going to the chapels; and lots of old terraced houses are being pulled down and replaced by modern developments.

There's hardly any work in South Wales these days, only mining, and that will probably be finishing soon. But the picture is not all bad. At least they have removed some of the old slag heaps that used to spoil the beautiful countryside around here.

There are some Welsh traditions that will probably never disappear. We still have the best rugby team in the world, who play at Cardiff Arms Park. I often go there to watch them. In June there is the miners' gala, also in Cardiff, the capital of Wales. Miners and their families from all over South Wales come to join in the processions and listen to the union speeches and play games. The big event is the jazz band festival. Every village has a band where children, mostly girls, dress up in smart uniforms and march to the sound of music.

"I know all the cows by name"

Tony Gregory is 48 and has been a farmer for thirty-two years. He owns a 60-hectare (150-acre) dairy farm with 280 head of cattle near Chippenham, Wiltshire.

I started off this farm in 1960 with just six heifers. Now we've got 280 head of cattle. Not all of them are in milk of course. Some are still heifers, but we do milk sixty-five cows a day. Together, they give us an average of 1,400 liters (370 gallons) of good quality butterfat milk every day. That's the best yield in the whole of the county. Almost all of it goes to the dairy at Melksham. A tank truck comes to collect it each morning. The milk is made into cream, yogurt and desserts. Because it is high in butterfat content and therefore richer and creamier, we get paid a bit extra for it. We get 15p per liter (23¢ per quart) at present as opposed to 12p per liter (18¢ per quart) for milk that goes for bottling.

I work the farm with my two sons and

Tony's milking shed is old-fashioned by modern standards.

Newborn calves can stand up soon after birth. This one is only two days old.

a lad who is on a government work experience scheme for six months. That is a scheme whereby the government pays employers to give work to unemployed youngsters. He came here to see if the farming life suited him. He's fitted in really well and I can't think how we got on without him.

Our day begins pretty early. By 6:15 a.m. we are all out in the fields bringing in the cows for their first milking of the day. Some farmers use dogs but I think they make the cows uneasy and affect the milk yield. I know all the cows by name and they know where to stand for the milking. Our milking shed is rather old-fashioned, but to replace it with a new parlour would cost about £80,000 ($120,000), and I'd lose contact with the cows. This way I can talk to them and pat them now and again and see exactly how they are getting on. It's well worth the extra hour it takes I think.

As well as milk, I also get an income from breeding cattle. I've got four bulls of my own. I bred them all here on the farm. Their ancestors came from a herd of British Friesians (Holsteins) in Bletchley, Buckinghamshire – probably the best herd in Britain. Now *we've* got one of the best. At present I've got seven cows in calf and three gave birth last week. The calves will be sold at the local market unless I keep them for myself. The bullocks will go for veal after being fattened and the heifers will be sold for milking.

During the summer the weather is good enough to keep the cattle out in the fields all day. I feed them a bit of cattle cake, but mostly they eat the natural grass. I'm lucky here because there is a good supply of water from the local brook, but I still have to use fertilizer on the fields. In the winter all the cows are kept in a cow shed – the fields would turn to mud if I left them out.

It's hard work being a farmer, but it's a healthy and enjoyable life. I can't imagine how terrible it would be to have to work inside all day long.

"We don't do it for the money"

Brian Brown is 35. He's an active crew member of the Angle lifeboat, operated by the Royal National Lifeboat Institution on the Pembrokeshire coast in South Wales. He has been a lifeboatman for sixteen years.

I've lived here in Angle most of my life and joined the Royal National Lifeboat Institution (R.N.L.I.) when I was just 19. I was operating a small ferry boat belonging to a hotel then, taking supplies and passengers to a small island,

The lifeboats of the R.N.L.I. are manned entirely by volunteers.

you understand. But that wasn't the life for me. I wanted to be my own boss. So I bought an old ship's lifeboat and refitted her out as a fishing boat myself, in the back garden. As a proper member of the fishing community it stood to reason that I should be an active member of the R.N.L.I.

The R.N.L.I. is a voluntary organization whose aim is to help ships and boats in distress on the sea. It was begun by Sir William Hillary on the Isle of Man in 1824. It doesn't receive a penny from the government. All the money is raised by donations and bequests from the public. The whole organization costs about £16 million a year to run. There are 200 lifeboat stations around the coast of Britain and they operate 130 big sea-going boats, like ours at Angle, and 129 smaller inflatable inshore boats.

The Angle lifeboat is called the *Richard Vernon and Mary Garforth of Leeds*, after two former patrons who left most of their money to the R.N.L.I. She

Brian manages to make a living from the lobsters he catches.

is built of solid timber and was first launched in 1957. She was refitted in 1981 with self-righting gear. Now if she rolled over in a really heavy sea she would come back up the right way. I just hope she doesn't do it when I'm on the crew!

Traditionally, the lifeboat crew were fishermen who were in the villages anyway during stormy weather, so they were available to man the lifeboats. Nowadays we have all sorts of people on the crew. Mostly these are self-employed people like butchers, builders and shopkeepers who work nearby to the lifeboat station. We are all notified of an emergency by maroons (flares) that are fired up across the village by the coxswain. He's the sort of captain of the lifeboat and he usually gets a phone call from the coastguard, although he does have a new radio now. We all drop what we're doing and rush down to the lifeboat.

Although most of us are voluntary members of the crew we do get our expenses paid by the R.N.L.I. But we don't do it for the money – somebody has to do it, and we're here you see.

Usually we have a crew of six or seven men and it takes only a few minutes to launch the boat down the steep ramp. I often take the wheel when we go out on a call because I'm used to it you see; it's part of my everyday job.

Most of the rescues we carry out from here are yachts that have got into trouble coming over from Ireland across St David's Channel. But in the summer we get a lot of stupid holidaymakers caught out in dinghies or canoes. They make us cross really because they know nothing about the sea and this area gets very rough in a southwesterly wind. Still, we can't let them drown can we!

When I'm not out on a call or practicing, as we do every six weeks, I'm mending my lobster pots or fishing them along the rugged Pembrokeshire coast. I've got one hundred pots and it's a good day if I catch a total of ten lobsters and a couple of crabs. I sell my fish to the local fish market at Milford and make a reasonable living from it.

"We do not normally carry guns"

Janet Lewis is 22. She is a woman police constable (W.P.C.) and lives and works at Milton Keynes, a new town about 100 km. (60 miles) north of London.

The police force as we know it was founded in this country in 1829. The policemen were nicknamed "Peelers" or "Bobbies" after Sir Robert Peel, the man who founded the force. There are two important differences between the British police force and those in other countries. In the first place we do not normally carry guns – they are only issued to us in very special circumstances. In the second place we are not a national force under the direct control of the government as are the police forces in France or Italy.

The police force in Britain is divided into forty-one small forces or "constabularies" as we call them. The Thames Valley force,

Janet meets a fellow officer while on a routine patrol around Milton Keynes.

which I work for, was formed in 1968 and is an amalgamation of five smaller constabularies – Buckinghamshire, Berkshire, Oxfordshire, Oxford City and Reading Borough. That is why our cap badge shows five crowns and a wavy line – the five old forces and the River Thames.

There are twenty police officers and five women police officers at Milton Keynes as well as an inspector and four sergeants. We work a sort of rota system so that there is usually a girl on in each shift. If I'm working nights I often drive a panda car (so-called because they are two colors) but during the day I'm usually on foot patrol, although I sometimes go out on a bicycle.

During the three years that I've been on the beat in Milton Keynes I've got to know a lot of different people. It's so nice to walk through the town, in or out of uniform, and to recognize and talk to so many of them. That's what police work is all about really – simply being seen to be a part of the community as a whole; making sure the public know that we are here to help them in whatever way we can. It's amazing how satisfying it is just to give simple directions to an elderly person when you realize how much they appreciate it. Sometimes they just want a chat about the weather or their son; it's all part of the job.

Most of the time we don't have a lot of serious crime here, although there is a lot of shoplifting from the stores in the new shopping center. Usually it's children, doing it for a dare, but we did catch one professional gang a little while ago.

Milton Keynes is a new town with a population of about 100,000 and seventy per cent of these are under forty years old. Although there is a village nearby

Janet always finds the time to stop and talk to the people she meets on the beat.

with the same name, the town was built from scratch to create relief housing and employment for people from London and the industrial north of England and Scotland.

When the town was first built people were reluctant to move here, but now that things are more settled and community centers, surgeries (medical facilities) and shops have been completed, the new residents seem happier. I certainly enjoy living and working here. Although the job as a woman police officer is not as glamorous as I thought it would be when I was a child, I'm glad to be helping people in a new community, like Milton Keynes, and can't think of another career that I'd rather have.

"Here in the glen there is no other industry"

John Robertson is 62. For twenty-five years he has worked at the Glen Livet distillery at Glen Livet, near Dufftown on the edge of the Grampian Highland region of Scotland.

There are two types of Scotch whiskey: malt and grain. Malt whiskey, which is what we produce here, is made from malted barley, grown locally. Grain whiskey has unmalted barley and maize added, so it's not so pure. There are 116 malt distilleries and 14 grain distilleries in Scotland. The Glenlivet was one of the first to be set up here. It was established in 1824. All the distilleries produce a different-tasting whiskey, even though the production process is almost identical at each of the places. Ours is one of the best of course; it's the wonderful water we use that gives it the taste! We produce nearly nine million liters (two million gallons) of whiskey each year.

When I started work here twenty-five years ago there were a lot more people working here than there are today. I can remember shoveling coal into the furnaces to heat the stills. Nowadays,

John is dwarfed by one of the giant copper stills at the Glenlivet distillery.

Thousands of deer roam the Grampian region.

it's all automatic and gas-fired so fewer staff are needed.

According to British law, Scotch whiskey has to be at least three years old before it can be sold. Ours is traditionally twelve years old. After the distilling process, the liquid is stored in oak casks called hogsheads until the time comes to bottle it. All our whiskey is sent down to Edinburgh to be bottled and blended. Blending whiskey is a very skilled job and entails mixing several different whiskeys together to achieve a perfect taste. Not all our whiskey is blended. The best is just bottled and called The Glenlivet. I used to drink it myself, but I liked it too much and so decided to become a teetotaler!

Here in the glen there is no other industry so the distilleries are a godsend. If it weren't for them we'd probably be out fishing in all weathers or chasing a few sheep around the hills. No, I like working and living here; I always have done. It's such an interesting place. Not many of the people here ever go far away, so when I was asked by the chairman of the company to accompany him to Buckingham Palace last year I thought he was joking! The Glenlivet distillery received the Queen's Award for Export. Scotland exports over 200 million liters (55 million gallons) of whiskey a year and earns nearly 800 million pounds for the British economy. Visiting and talking to the Queen was a marvelous experience, and I wouldn't have missed it for the world.

This part of Scotland is well known for its good fishing and shooting. There are large estates all along the River Spey and people come from all over Britain to fish for the famous Spey salmon or to shoot the grouse up on the moors. Recently the deer have become a nuisance, so many more of them have had to be culled. It seems a shame, but that's the way of life here.

"As a Moslem I believe that everybody is equal"

Guftar Hussein is 32. He came to Britain from Pakistan in 1965 with his family and now owns a store selling all kinds of produce for the Asian community in Slough, Berkshire.

Like a great number of Pakistanis, I came to Britain to find work in the mid-1960s. Before then very few of us had thought of coming over, but the British Government invited us to work in the factories and we were tempted by the promised housing and employment. Pakistan is a poor country by comparison. Now many of us are returning to our home country because of the social unrest, the lack of employment and the racial hatred. But I am not bitter about this – there are bad people in the world wherever one goes. We get on well with most British people.

There are many thousands of Indians and Pakistanis in this country. They practice all the religions of our continent. There are Hindus, Sikhs and many others. We are Moslems, like most of the people from Pakistan. The vast majority of us live in the industrial Midlands in towns like Nottingham, Sheffield and Leicester. But we chose

Guftar's store specializes in produce for the Asian community of Slough.

to come to Slough, in the south of England, to open our shop.

We cater for all tastes here. We sell many different vegetables from India and Pakistan like green chilies, white radishes, brinjals (eggplant), bitter melons, okra and lots of beans from the east coast of Africa, where a lot of my countrymen have settled in the past. We also sell all kinds of pulses, they're dried beans, dhal and lentils, as well as Pakistani biscuits, pickles and chapati flour.

The Moslem god is Allah. We believe that Jesus Christ was a prophet of Allah, but not his son. As a Moslem I believe that everybody, whatever his color, race, or creed, is equal. A good Moslem is a good man. We pray to Allah five times a day — once in the morning before dawn, twice during the day and twice after sunset. Friday is our holy day and then we go to the mosque to pray and meet our friends.

All of my children go to the normal state schools. They integrate really well with the white children; there is no doubt about that. After school they always go to the mosque to learn the scriptures from the Holy Koran — our Bible, if you like. They also learn to speak Urdu, one of the main languages of Pakistan. I speak Urdu and Punjabi as well as English, but some of my customers can speak Gujarati as well.

A great many British people think that our marriages are arranged like those in the Hindu religion. In fact the Moslem faith gives us the choice of marrying whomever we wish to. However, a lot of us do get married very young and often our partners are suggested to us by our parents.

I got married in Pakistan when I was 16. My wife was 16 too. Although she was chosen for me I did meet her many times during the six months or so before we got married.

We make a good living from our shop

Although Moslems are a minority in Britain they have built many beautiful mosques around the country.

here in Slough. We work hard, employ four people, and open for twelve hours a day. But I do look forward to my trips back to Pakistan, to Rawalpindi, high up in the mountains near Kashmir, where my parents still live the peasant way of life.

"Palm trees flourish here in Northern Ireland"

Arthur Robinson is 54. He works as a manager for the Harland and Woolf shipyard in Belfast, the capital of Northern Ireland. He lives at Bangor, a seaside resort on the shores of Belfast Lough.

Ships have been built here in Belfast for hundreds of years but my company started only in 1859. In that year Edward J. Harland, a Yorkshireman, bought a small shipyard from a Mr. Hickson. Two years later Harland took a partner, Gustav Woolf, and so the present company of Harland and Woolf was founded. In the early days we built mostly sailing ships but later on we began adding engines. Many of the great liners of the past were built here in Belfast but now we concentrate mainly on giant tankers, bulk carriers and liquefied-gas carriers.

My job in the contracts management department is to see that the ships we build will perform the functions expected of them and also conform to the very rigid specifications laid down when they are ordered. This is no easy task when you consider that a large ship is made up of hundreds of thousands of pieces of steel, plus engines, generators, control systems and components of all shapes and sizes. These are delivered to the shipyard from over 750 different specialist firms.

We like to think that we build some of the best ships in the world here. At the present time there are about 170 operating on the high seas that were built in the

Arthur discusses the plans for a new ship with a shipyard worker.

The history of British shipbuilding dates back hundreds of years.

Belfast shipyard. Among these are the two largest tankers ever constructed in the U.K., the 323,000-ton *Coastal Corpus Christi*, and *Coastal Hercules*. We have also recently completed a series of car ferries, so if you ever travel between France and England on a Sealink ferry you may well travel on a Harland and Woolf-built ship.

Building ships in Belfast is no easy task: all our raw materials – steel, timber, chains and springs – have to be imported. Here in Northern Ireland we have an oceanic climate with frequent rain showers in both winter and summer. The summers are never really hot so we have to do a lot of our painting indoors. This, of course, means that we have to spend a fortune building huge sheds. The only real advantage that we have here is that we get very little frosty weather. The Gulf Stream flows from the Caribbean up and around Northern Ireland and gives us quite mild winters – in fact palm trees flourish here!

At the moment it is very difficult for us to keep all 7,000 of our men in work. The increase in oil prices in 1974 caused many people to economize in their use of oil. The number of tankers needed in the world has dropped sharply and shipowners are no longer ordering this type of vessel.

In addition, of course, many countries, like Yugoslavia, Spain, Brazil and South Korea, have set up shipyards of their own and no longer buy from Britain. So far, however, they are building only simple ships and that is why we are concentrating on very complicated ships like gas carriers. Harland and Woolf have a reputation for introducing new ideas into ships and ship-building methods and this is more than ever necessary if we are to stay ahead of our competitors.

"Ninety per cent of the lessons are in Welsh"

Brede Arkless comes from Dublin in the Republic of Ireland. Now she lives and works with her husband and eight children at Llanberis, a tiny village in Snowdonia, North Wales.

Back in 1970 my husband Geoff and I decided to set up a climbing school here in Snowdonia National Park. Although I come from Dublin, I found that I was spending a good deal of my time over here climbing. So we came to live in Llanberis, the center for climbing in North Wales.

It wasn't easy at first to get established, but now the school is reasonably well known and we keep busy throughout the year. We run courses in rock climbing, mountaineering, canoeing and orienteering. When the weather is terrible, as it often is, we go off potholing in the local disused lead or slate mines.

The area attracts many thousands of people throughout the year. Some come with their friends to climb on the rocky crags above the glacial valley of the Pass of Llanberis; others come and join a school like ours to learn new skills or to perfect old ones. There are about six schools here

Brede climbs one of the more difficult crags high above the road through the Pass of Llanberis in North Wales.

Once completed, the Dinorwic power station will be the largest of its kind in the world.

and the Sports Council of Great Britain supports a large one over the pass at Capel Curig called Plas Y Brenin.

Some of the best climbing in Europe is to be found here above the pass. Top class climbers from all over the world come here to practice for the Alps, Andes and the Himalayas. It is very dangerous, though, and every year there are fatal accidents on Snowdon. At 1,085 m. (3,560 ft.) it is the highest mountain in England and Wales. It looks so easy in the sunshine, with its well-defined tracks, but when the mists come down it is treacherous and people just get lost or fall down the steep scree slopes.

Ten years ago we used to climb on Dinorwic, a slate crag the other side of the lake, across from the village. But now the Central Electricity Generating Board have bought the land and are about to complete the largest pumped-water power station in the world. The powerhouse is underground and it is as big as two soccer pitches and as high as a fourteen-story building! It is the largest man-made hole in the world. They've removed more than three million tons of rock to dig it. When it's finished, the power station will supply over 1,600 MW of electricity to the national grid for up to five hours. Then it will pump all the water back up to the reservoir that has been built at the top of the mountain. It's a shame about the climbing, but the power station itself will attract valuable tourists into the area in the future.

Most of this part of Wales is Welsh speaking. I had to send my children into Bangor, about 30 km (18 miles) away, to school. Here in Llanberis, ninety per cent of the school lessons are in Welsh and none of my children could speak it when we arrived, although some of the younger ones are now picking up the odd word. It's a very difficult language to learn unless you are brought up with it I think. It was dying out a few years ago but there has been a great revival recently, and many TV and radio programs are in Welsh now.

"The British are great beer drinkers"

John Tribble is 39. He owns a small country public house (pub) – the Ring O'Bells – in Chagford, a village in the heart of the Dartmoor National Park in Devon.

I'm always up by 6:30, checking the shelves in the bar of the Ring O' Bells and cleaning the cellar where I keep the beer. The beer has to be stored somewhere cool to keep it in good condition. The pub is a rambling old building. According to local records it dates from the eleventh century.

It's called the Ring O' Bells because one of the previous owners was a bell ringer at the village church.

The pub is what's called a "free house".

The pub is the social center and meeting place for people in towns and villages throughout the length and breadth of Britain.

A typical misty start to the day and Chagford village on Dartmoor.

That means it is not tied to any particular brewery. I can buy my beers, wines and spirits from whatever source I choose. Most pubs in Britain are tied to a brewery, so the tenant landlord or manager has no choice at all as to his supplier. I sell four different brews of beer: the most popular is Harvest Bitter.

The British are great beer drinkers. Beer is drunk in pint (0.5 liter) or half-pint glasses, and we consume about 31 million pints (17.5 million liters) a day from the 200 breweries all over the country. These days lots of people are drinking wine as well, so gone are the days when a publican in this country could make a healthy living from selling beer alone.

Since we moved into the pub my wife, Dot, has become very keen on the food side of the business. People coming into a pub these days expect to have a bite to eat with their drink, and Dot does them really proud. We do lots of traditional English dishes like roast beef and Yorkshire pudding, fresh Dartmoor trout, and steak and kidney pie. We've just finished extending the little restaurant so we can seat nearly thirty people now.

Our busiest time is lunchtime. Because of the licensing laws in this country, I am only allowed to open between 10:30 and 2:30 over lunch and between 5:30 and 10:30 during the evening, although this is extended to 11:00 at the weekends. Some people think that pubs should stay open all the afternoon like the bars on the Continent. But it already costs me £4,000 ($6,000) a year to run this place. If I had to pay staff to come in the afternoon as well I just couldn't afford to stay here.

Traditionally the English pub is the focal point of town and village life – a place where people can meet for a drink and a chat and a game of darts, cards or dominoes with their friends. Although most of my regular customers are folk from the sheep farming community, Dartmoor National Park, in the heart of England's "West Country," does attract walkers and holiday-makers from all over Britain. It is one of the many national parks in Britain and must be one of the few remaining places where you can enjoy beautiful unspoiled countryside during the day and end up in a friendly old pub like this one!

"I do more than just deliver letters"

Nigel Nice is 31 and a postman on a remote part of Skye, an island off the west coast of Scotland. He lives in the tiny village of Elgol, which is 24 km. (15 miles) from the nearest town.

There's been a system for delivering mail in Britain for hundreds of years, but the first postage stamp was not issued until 1840. The postal system is operated by the Post Office, which has its headquarters in London, and hundreds of smaller post offices and sub-post offices in towns and villages all over the country. Now the Post Office employs about 170,000 people and handles around 100 million letters and parcels every year.

Here on Skye, though, I do more than just deliver letters and parcels. There is no public transportation system on this part of the island so the post office operates a limited passenger service as well. The bus that I drive has eleven seats and allows people from the outlying farms and hamlets to get into Broadford for shopping or for work. Although it's the largest town for miles, it's only got a choice of three grocers' shops.

As there is no public transportation system on some parts of Skye, Nigel has to carry passengers as well as mail.

I live in Elgol, a tiny village on the southwest coast of the island. I pick up my postbus at Elgol post office every morning at 8 a.m. and drive the 24 km. (15 miles) to Broadford, picking up passengers and emptying the five post boxes at intervals along the road.

I also pick up the school children that live along my route and take them to the junior (elementary) school in Broadford. There's an infants' school in Elgol, but older children have to travel into the town.

There are only fifty deliveries, or drops, as we call them, on my entire round, but sometimes it takes me about three hours to complete. I take groceries to some of the elderly people; I deliver the milk and newspapers six days a week; and there are often pieces of machinery for some of the farmers. Often too I pass on messages for those people who don't like writing letters! I'm not supposed to deliver livestock, but the occasional puppy or rabbit does find its way onto the bus. The Post Office charges people, of course, for all these extra services. It's 70p ($1.05) to travel from Elgol to Broadford and it costs 10p (15¢) to have a pint of milk delivered.

At the moment I rent the little crofter's cottage where I live, but my wife and I are hoping to be able to buy a bit of land soon to build our own house. It's often very cold and wet here on Skye and we all burn peat on our fires to keep warm. There's no coal or wood on the island so the locals have been using peat for generations. Each croft has its own peat bog nearby. I've just learned how to cut and dry it in the age-old way. It's all part of living here.

People often ask me how I put up with the isolation of living here on Skye, especially since I was brought up in the city. Well, it's difficult to explain, but out here I feel part of the living community; it's good to know that you are helping people and I suppose there's a sense of belonging to something really. I'd hate to live in the city again.

Few trees can grow on Skye so peat has been used as fuel for centuries.

"The only regular Hovercraft service in the world"

Tony Quaife is 34. He lives in Kent and is a Hovercraft captain with a newly formed company called Hoverspeed, which links the English ports of Ramsgate and Dover with Calais and Boulogne in France.

Hovercraft began regular crossings of the English Channel in 1969. I became a Hovercraft captain four years later. There were two companies then: Hoverlloyd, the one I worked for, and one called Seaspeed, operated and owned by the state railway company, British Rail.

About two years ago they amalgamated and formed one company called Hoverspeed. We now operate out of both Ramsgate and the new terminal at Dover. We go to Calais and Boulogne over in France, and each of our six craft can do as many as seven crossings in a day. There are four Hovercraft that work out of Dover, so that's an average of one crossing every twenty minutes or so.

We run the only regular Hovercraft service in the world. There is a lot of interest in this form of transportation in both the U.S.A. and the U.S.S.R., but as yet Britain is way ahead. We can take as

Britain is less than half an hour from the Continent by Hovercraft.

The massive port complex at Dover, where sea passengers arrive and depart for the Continent.

many as 418 passengers and 55 cars on the big Hovercraft that I'm in charge of. Often we take fewer cars but include about half a dozen coaches instead. We carry upwards of two million passengers a year.

When the seas are calm we can cover the 35 km. (22 miles) from Dover to Calais in twenty-eight minutes, traveling at an average of 100 k.p.h. (60 m.p.h.). When it's rough we have to cut our speed and it takes about an hour.

Although we call our journey across the Channel a "flight," it's only a convenient term really. We have to deal with all the hazards of the sea, not those of the air. We are just like a ferry really, but much more maneuverable. The English Channel is the busiest waterway in the world, with many thousands of ships passing up and down the sea lanes during the year.

There are other hazards too, apart from shipping. When we cross out of Ramsgate we often go across Goodwin Sands, way out in the Channel. They dry out at low tide and we go right over them. It's our only chance to operate the Hovercraft on dry land except at the beginning and end of our crossings! But when the weather is bad and it's half tide, the seas can be incredibly rough and we have to avoid the area.

Many of our passengers go over to France to visit the French supermarkets and to buy cheap food. It seems strange to me, but since Britain joined the European Economic Community (E.E.C.) in 1973, food prices have risen dramatically. There are some things like cheese and wine that are very much cheaper in France than they are in Britain. If you buy enough the saving pays for your day out! I just hope that people will continue to travel by Hovercraft and keep me in a job.

"Shakespeare is Britain's best-known playwright"

Josette Simon is 23. She is an actress with the Royal Shakespeare Company. She came originally from Leicester, but now lives and works in Stratford-upon-Avon, Shakespeare's birthplace and the home of the company.

I came here to Stratford in February 1982. Prior to that, I'd been on stage at the Haymarket in Leicester and had acted on TV. Although I enjoy TV drama, I find that acting in front of a live audience is much more stimulating and exciting. So when my contract with the TV company ran out I came in search of work back on the stage. Over ninety per cent of all the trained actors and actresses in Britain are out of work at any one time, so I was very lucky to be offered a contract with the Royal Shakespeare Company (R.S.C.).

Shakespeare is Britain's best-known playwright. He was born in 1564 and wrote thirty-seven plays as well as many poems. Visitors come from all over the world to see his birthplace here at Stratford-upon-Avon in Warwickshire. They also come to see the cottage in which his wife, Anne Hathaway, was born. That is in Shottery, a village just a few kilometers from Stratford.

The Shakespeare Memorial Theatre was completed in Stratford in 1879. It later burned down but was replaced in 1932 with the present building, which was opened by the then Prince of Wales on 23rd April — the day on which Shakespeare is thought to have been born. The theater was renamed the Royal Shakespeare Theatre.

The Royal Shakespeare Company itself was formed in 1960, although its history dates back to 1769. In that year a man called David Garrick presented a festival of acting, music and revelry to the local inhabitants of Stratford. Now it is one of the largest and most famous theater companies in the world and plays to an audience of over a million people every year. The company tours annually to Newcastle in the north of England and to many small towns and villages that have no resident professional theater company of their own. In 1982 the company moved into additional premises at the Barbican Centre in the City of London.

Although the R.S.C. probably attracts larger audiences than any theater

Josette applies her makeup before going on the stage of the Royal Shakespeare Theatre.

company in the world, it is impossible to finance the vastly expensive productions that we put on from ticket sales alone. So, like so many of the 270 professional theater companies in Britain, we rely on the Arts Council of Great Britain to provide for about a third of our costs. Like other theater companies, too, we receive a certain amount of help through sponsorship from industry and from TV coverage of our plays.

I love working as an actress but it is very hard work indeed. I spend a lot of my time learning my lines or rehearsing on the stage. I don't only act in plays by William Shakespeare, though. This year I'll be appearing in *Peer Gynt* by Henrik Ibsen and *Lear* by Edward Bond, as well as Shakespeare's *Macbeth, The Tempest, The Taming of the Shrew, Anthony and Cleopatra, King Lear* and *Much Ado About Nothing*. Most of the parts are quite small at the moment, but when I'm a little older I hope to tackle some of the bigger and more ambitious parts.

The Royal Shakespeare Theatre in Stratford-upon-Avon, the town where the great poet and playwright was born in 1564.

"Tomato seed is dearer than gold"

Philip Duffy is 32. He and his father own and operate over thirty-six hectares (ninety acres) of market garden on two sites near Boston, in Lincolnshire.

The land around here is marvelous. The flat landscape and stone-free, alluvial soil make the Cambridgeshire fens and Lincolnshire one of the most productive farming areas in the whole world. Much of the land here was reclaimed by Dutch farmers hundreds of years ago. They used it for rearing sheep which is why a lot of the back roads are so windy – they follow the sheep tracks of old.

Market gardening, the growing of fruit and vegetables for market, has changed radically over the past few years. It's become highly automated and highly competitive. The seeds are planted by machine and the germinating plants are watered and fertilized by machine. Now that Britain is a

Potatoes are grown in vast quantities on the flat, fertile land of Lincolnshire.

member of the E.E.C., we have to compete not just with other British market gardeners but with the Europeans too. People nowadays expect to be able to buy fresh vegetables and flowers all the year round and not just in the summer.

My father and I work about thirty-six hectares (ninety acres). A good deal of this land is put down to wheat, potatoes and cut flowers, like daffodils and tulips. My father looks after that pretty well on his own. I concentrate on the two hectares (five acres) or so of glasshouses (greenhouses) that I've built over the last few years. It was a huge investment even though I did receive a small grant from the E.E.C.

Some of the market gardeners around here specialize in producing peas and green beans for canning and freezing. Big food companies even own and operate their own market gardens. I grow mostly what we call brassicas – cabbages, Brussels sprouts and cauliflowers. I raise the plants from seed and then sell them when they are about 15 cm. (6 inches) high to the big commercial growers who mature them in their fields for sale to wholesalers, shops and supermarkets.

Most of the seed I use comes from Holland or Australia. Both countries specialize in producing high-yield seed. It's probably the best seed in the world but it is very expensive. A kilo of Brussels sprout seed costs me over £400 ($270 a pound); cauliflower seed costs more than £250 a kilo ($168 a pound). As for tomato seed, that is dearer than gold for a given weight!

The produce from the commercial growers that I supply goes from Lincolnshire to places all over the country, as well as to the local markets. A lot of it goes to the New Covent Garden market in London – one of the largest and most famous flower, fruit and vegetable markets in the

Philip transplants one of the hundreds of tomato plants that he grows from seed.

world. From there it is distributed around Britain and the world. Much of it goes straight to the large industrial areas of the Midlands and the north of England.

Market gardening is a full-time job and February is the only month I get any time off. It's the coldest month of the year up here. We suffer badly from frost in the winter and although I don't use heaters in the glasshouses I do use warm air blowers on the coldest nights. Last winter the temperature dropped to -25°C. (-13°F.) and all the soil in the glasshouses froze, even with the blowers on!

"Scotland is so beautiful it almost sells itself"

Jean Duncan is 55. She lives in Edinburgh, the capital of Scotland. Jean works as a freelance tourist guide with the Scottish Tourist Guides Association and has traveled to nearly every part of Scotland.

There are about one hundred tourist guides working for the Scottish Tourist Guides Association in Edinburgh and another thirty or so in Glasgow. Every year we look after thousands of visitors, both from Britain and abroad. Most of the guides are full time but I only work six months of the year.

With its mountains, rivers and lochs, Scotland is so beautiful it almost sells itself. All I have to do is to fill in the details

Jean greets another coach party of tourists outside the castle in Edinburgh.

of history and geography. Most of my time is spent traveling around the country on a coach telling the touring passengers about the history of the many castles and other places of interest that we pass on the road.

I especially enjoy the trips to the Highlands. There we visit Culloden, where Charles Edward Stuart, or Bonny Prince Charlie, the Scottish rebel, was crushed by the supporters of King George II in 1749. Then there's Loch Ness, of course. I always keep a little plastic monster in my bag to show the children what we think he is like!

The Highland Games at Braemar is always a popular event to take people to. They are held on the first Saturday in September every year and visitors can see all the traditional Scottish sports – putting the shot, throwing the hammer and, most famous of all, tossing the caber. Nearly all the competitors wear a kilt, which really pleases the foreign tourists.

Although I enjoy showing people all over Scotland, my favorite place is Edinburgh. There is so much to see in the capital of Scotland. Not only do we have some of the best shops in the country, but we have a castle overflowing with history dating back to the eleventh century. It is where Mary Queen of Scots was kept for her own safety when her life was threatened by the sixteenth-century Protestants encouraged by John Knox and Queen Elizabeth I of England. Edinburgh also boasts the Palace of Holyroodhouse where the present Queen Elizabeth stays when she visits the city.

Every August there is the Edinburgh Festival with its exhibitions of art and its hundreds of "fringe" shows of theater, film and other performing arts that have become as well-known as the main festival itself.

During the summer months I take visitors on evening walks through the city, often down the "Royal Mile" that stretches from the castle gates down through the old city. Along the road, with its many side alleys and lanes, the houses and churches seem full of the history of our ancestors. The walks usually end up in a hotel where the visitors can sample the delights of haggis, shortbread and Scotch whiskey while they listen to the music of bagpipes. Some visitors will even have a try at playing this traditional Scottish instrument themselves. The evening usually ends up with a Ceilidh (pronounced kay-lee), where we all dance and sing traditional Scottish songs. It's the sort of thing that most tourists come to see and we don't like to see them go away disappointed.

Edinburgh, the capital of Scotland, is steeped in history dating back to the eleventh century.

"One of the biggest cities in the world"

Pat Navin is 45. He came over to England from the Republic of Ireland in 1957. He drives one of London Transport's famous double-decker red buses through the busy streets of Britain's capital city.

The first buses ran in London in 1829. They were horse-drawn. Buses using petrol (gas) arrived much later, in 1897. Of course, the streets of London were much less busy then than they are today. Now London Transport, under the control of the Greater London Council, operates over 6,500 buses throughout the London area. They travel 280 million km. (175 million miles) every year carrying 1,190 million passengers!

The bus I drive takes people from Highgate, one of the northern suburbs of London, to Moorgate in the City. It's a very busy route, particularly during the "rush hours." That is what we call the periods between about 8 and 9:30 a.m. and 4:30 and 6 p.m. They are the times when most people travel to and from work.

Although many people think of the whole of London as the city, in fact the City of London covers only a very small area north of the River Thames. It is where the Bank of England, the Stock Exchange and many of the other important financial institutions are located.

Many of the streets in London now have bus lanes, which only buses are allowed to use at certain times of the day. These have helped to speed up the bus service, but you still need a lot of patience when you are driving around London. It is one of the busiest cities in the world and every day there are holdups due to roadworks or just heavy traffic.

People who want to travel around London quickly can use the Underground (subway), or the "tube" as Londoners call it. The Underground is also run by London Transport and the Greater London Council, and is one of the largest and most comprehensive underground railway systems in the world. There are nine lines making up the system and 279 stations connected by 420 km. (260 miles) of track.

I take about £70–£80 ($100–120) a day in fares. People who travel regularly can buy a season ticket which allows them to travel anywhere in London for a given period – a week, a month or a year, for example. Old-age pensioners (men over 65 or women over 60) can travel free on the buses except during the rush hours.

The bus service in Britain's capital city is subsidized through rates and taxes.

Although many millions of people every year use London Transport's buses and trains, the total amount of revenue from fares is insufficient to cover the cost of running the services. So the Greater London Council subsidizes the transport system through the rates, which are local taxes charged against the people who live in London.

A lot of people think that driving a bus must be a very boring job, but there is always something going on in the London streets to interest me. Bus driving wouldn't suit everybody but I wouldn't be a driver if I didn't enjoy it.

The London Underground was the first subway system in the world and was completed in 1863.

"Most secondary schools are comprehensive"

Peter Hesketh is 55. An engineer for most of his life, Peter now teaches art to children at Aireborough Grammar School in Leeds, Yorkshire, in the north of England.

Here at Aireborough we have 950 children and 55 teachers, which is probably about average for a secondary school in Britain. The school is called a grammar school *(see Glossary)* but it is in fact comprehensive. Until recently, most secondary schools in Britain were selective. At age 11 children took a test that determined which type of school – grammar, technical or secondary modern – they went to. Now the number of grammar schools in Britain is declining and most secondary schools are comprehensive, taking children of all abilities from age 11 to 16. Aireborough became a comprehensive school in 1976. I think the comprehensive system is much fairer for the kids: they all get the same chance of success with their exams.

I'm one of half a million teachers in Britain and have been teaching for nine years. At 46, I was rather late entering the profession. I teach art – or I am supposed to! I don't think that you can really teach art, only encourage it. Every kid has the potential to succeed. It's up to the teacher to recognize it and then help it along. I get a real mixed bag of children into my classroom, but they are all good at art – or think they are, and that's all that matters to them!

The art class at Aireborough. The children's paintings are exhibited around the walls.

Most schools in Britain provide subsidized meals for the children at noon.

All parents in Britain are obliged by law to send their children to school between the ages of 5 and 16. Most of the schools are like this one and are run by the state through local authorities. Education is by far the biggest item on any local authority budget. In total, about £8,000 million ($12 billion) a year is spent on educating the eleven million young people in our 32,000 schools.

Some schools though are privately owned and supported by the parents who send their children there. These schools are called private or public schools. Lots of schools are owned and run by the Catholic Church.

Secondary school children can take one of two sets of examinations at age 16. They can either take Certificates of Secondary Education (C.S.E.s) or General Certificates of Education at Ordinary Level (G.C.E. "O" levels). At 18, they can take G.C.E. "A" (advanced) levels which allow them to go to college or university.

I have to teach C.S.E. and "O" level art and "A" level art history here at Aireborough. We also run a school magazine from the art department. It's called *Graphos* and we use it to try to generate interest in school activities in the local area. The kids design it, write it, illustrate it, print it and distribute it. It's run on business lines and teaches the kids all about deadlines and management as well as layout and content. It's a great success and I think every school in the country should have one.

"Most visitors ask us about the monster"

Eveline Sabin is 46. For twenty-six years she and her husband have run the Lovat Arms Hotel. The hotel is situated at Ford Augustus on Loch Ness, in the heart of the Scottish Highlands.

There has been a hotel here for around 120 years, although it was originally a hunting lodge. It was built on the site of an old fort; you can still see a wall down by the kitchen garden. My father bought the hotel in 1947. When my husband Jack and I got married, we took it over with my sister Jan. My mother is chairman, so it's still very much a family business. Jack is the manager; I'm the cook. I've always enjoyed working in the kitchens. Jan does all the accounts and book work and we seem to work very well as a team.

Our busiest time is during the summer and at Christmas and New Year, when we get a lot of visitors to the Highlands. In Scotland, we call the New Year Hogmanay and it is much more of a celebration than Christmas. There's always Scottish dancing and merrymaking in the hotel. We have people from all over the world – Australia, South Africa, Germany and France. They all enjoy themselves so much; and so do we!

There's also the fishing, either on Loch Ness or on nearby Loch Oich. The salmon fishing season begins in January here and we always get people up from England to stay with us then. Just recently, over the past five years or so, we've got a lot of trade from the cruise boats that are hired out all along the Caledonian Canal from Inverness to Fort William away to the west of us. Thomas Telford, the famous engineer, did us a good turn when he built the canal in the early 1800s!

We get an average of twenty people a night to stay throughout the year. Altogether, that's over 7,000 beds to make! We employ eleven permanent staff, but that number rises to about twenty during the summer. Of course not everyone can afford to stay in a hotel, and we get quite a number of people who come in if the weather is bad just to have a meal or a shower. Well, they may not spend very much but we hope that when they come back to the area they'll come to stay here for a few days at least.

Most visitors to the hotel ask us about the famous Loch Ness monster. I don't believe in it myself, but our barman, Hamish, swears he saw it when he was a lad! It's strange that something that may not exist brings us such a lot of trade! People come here from all over the world in the hope of seeing "the beastie" as it is known locally. But even with so many people visiting the Glen, the local craftsmen are finding it difficult to make a living. It's so expensive just to live up here in this part of the Highlands.

Most years Jack and I try to get away to the sunshine for a while. We close the hotel for six weeks and just lie on a beach in the Mediterranean or somewhere where it's hot. It's so good to have a complete rest, and to get away from the cold Scottish winters, but I always look forward to getting back to work.

Roast beef is one of the favorite dishes at the Lovat Arms Hotel.

Using the Caledonian Canal, pleasure boat owners can travel from one side of Scotland to the other entirely by water.

"Settlers kept the traditional folk songs alive"

Don Morgan is 45. He lives in Bracknell, Berkshire, where he runs the local folk club. Both he and his wife Sarah have jobs during the day, but in their spare time they sing traditional English folk songs.

Sarah, my wife, and I have been running the folk club in Bracknell since 1975. We sing together regularly in pubs and clubs all over the south of England and are both members of a folk group called "Curate's Egg." Singing is for us though, only a spare-time activity and we both have to earn a living by working at other jobs during the day.

You don't necessarily need to play a complicated musical instrument to be a folksinger. Sarah and I perform a lot of our songs unaccompanied. I do play the clarinet, though, and Sarah plays the dulcimer sometimes. Although the guitar is by far the most popular instrument in folk music today neither Sarah nor I play it very much.

Many of the songs we sing today are English in origin but were collected in America by an English clergyman called Cecil Sharp, who went to the U.S.A. in the late nineteenth century. He came back with the songs taken there by the early settlers. Cut off from the outside world, the settlers kept the traditional English folk songs alive.

Cecil Sharp House in London is now the headquarters of the English Song and Dance Society. It houses a vast collection of songs gathered by Sharp and others. Anyone can go along to

Don and Sarah sing in the warm atmosphere of the Bracknell folk club.

A women's Morris team dances in the street to the accompaniment of accordians and drum.

Cecil Sharp House and learn a song, but many professional and amateur singers write their own material. Some folk groups – like Steeleye Span and Pentangle – have tried to break into the pop music charts by using electric violins and other electric instruments to play folk music.

Folk festivals have become more and more popular over the past few years. The biggest one is held every year at Sidmouth in Devon and attracts many thousands of people. We have one at Bracknell and both Sarah and I get very involved in this. Apart from the singing it's the wonderful social life that goes with the folk scene that Sarah and I enjoy. Over the past few years we have traveled to clubs throughout the country to sing both by invitation, or simply dropping in. We get paid for an invited session, but it's usually only enough to cover our expenses. Getting around is so expensive that amateurs and professionals alike find it difficult to travel far nowadays. Accommodation is no problem though: we take sleeping bags and someone at the club we are visiting always has a spare bed.

English folk music is often associated with a form of dance called a Morris dance. Morris dancing is really an ancient fertility rite to celebrate the coming of spring on 1st May. Originally, the dance was only performed by men, but now there are many Morris teams of men and women throughout the country. Each region has its own dances, but the basic idea is similar. Accompanied by drums and accordians, the dancers jump high in the air to make the corn grow and the bells sewn on to their costumes and the handkerchiefs they wave ward off the evil spirits of winter, and welcome the good spirits of spring.

"Most M.P.s have another job to do"

Keith Best is 32. He has been the Conservative Member of Parliament for Anglesey, an island off the coast of North Wales, since 1979. When first elected, at 29, he was the second youngest M.P. ever to sit in the House of Commons.

I am a barrister by profession and still run a practice in Brighton, down on the south coast. Most M.P.s have another job to do and some of us work as many as sixteen hours a day. The British system of government is somewhat complicated. At one time our sovereign, now Her Majesty Queen Elizabeth II, had absolute power over government. But now the monarch acts only on the advice from the government elected by his or her subjects.

There are two parts to the British Parliament. The House of Lords is made up of peers most of whom inherited their position. The House of Commons is made up of 650 M.P.s like myself who have been elected by the majority of people over 18 in this country – the voters. The job of both Houses is the same, however: to pass laws and make funds available to the many ministries and civil service departments.

There are three main political parties in Britain: the Labour Party, the Social Democratic Party in alliance with the Liberal Party, and the Conservative Party.

Every five years there is a general election. All the constituencies have their own local election, and the people in each constituency vote for the person that they think will best represent them in Parliament. The candidate with the most votes becomes the M.P. for that constituency and the party with the most M.P.s elected becomes the government for the next five years. The leader of that party becomes the Prime Minister and he or she chooses a group of M.P.s from the winning party to become the "Cabinet." These men and women then become the ministers for the various government departments such as trade, the environment, transport and education.

My job as a backbench M.P. (not in the Cabinet) is mainly concerned with my own electorate; that is, my constituents in Anglesey. But I am also on various committees. One is concerned with alcoholism in Britain and another with the plight of Vietnamese refugees. Some M.P.s have also been elected to represent Britain in the European Parliament since we joined the E.E.C.

The Houses of Parliament in London – the headquarters of the government of Britain.

Because I am forced to live in a flat in Westminster during the week, I can only get to Anglesey at the weekends. I advertise in the local newspapers the times of my visits and meet people in a caravan (trailer) that I tow to a different location every weekend. There is nothing to stop people visiting me at the House of Commons, of course; they only have to make an appointment and turn up. Some of the people who visit me in the caravan are elderly ladies having problems with their pensions; others are high-powered businessmen who talk of investing millions of pounds in industry. Each is as important as the other to an M.P.

I have been elected as a representative of the people and as such I have to exercise my own judgment as to the importance of any one matter. So no problem is too small or too large to discuss openly in the House of Commons. One minute it may be the price of crude oil in the Middle East; the next the pension of my elderly lady.

Keith Best and his assistant discuss the forthcoming day's events in Parliament.

"Our catch is worth £250,000"

Fred Harding is 49. He's been a fisherman working out of Hull for the past twenty-nine years and has seen many changes in the British fishing industry during that time.

Things have changed since I started fishing twenty-nine years ago. There used to be over two hundred boats working out of Hull – now there are about ten. The others are tied up at the dockside just rusting away or have been cut up for scrap.

I can remember in the 1950s when ten boats would go off together to the fishing grounds off Newfoundland or Iceland. There we caught mostly cod, but also haddock, coley, skate, plaice and dogfish. We went off in all weathers in much smaller boats than we've got now. We still fish the North Atlantic of course but since the fishing limits were extended in 1976 to about 320 km. (200 miles) around most countries finding fish has been more difficult. We have to have special licenses and every year a quota is set for each country.

I work for British United Trawlers. We are based in Grimsby, across the Humber estuary, but we work six boats from Hull. I'm a deckhand on the 1,000 ton *Roman*, built in Glasgow in 1974. It's like a palace compared to the little boats we used to put to sea in. There is even a TV on board, and video! She has a crew of eighteen men and eight officers, and we carry enough fuel, water and food for a hundred days at sea. When we are fishing we never stop – the nets are emptied and recast straight away while the catch is being processed and frozen.

We also fish the coast of Cornwall and Ireland for mackerel when they are in season. Sometimes there are so many of them that we catch fifty tons in one cast. Most of them go to Nigeria where they are used for fertilizer as well as for food. I can remember when we were catching nearly that weight of herrings off the coast of Scotland and northern England. In the early 1900s a whole secondary industry grew up around the herring fishing. People would travel from port to port following the big catches. They were employed to gut the fish and to make the barrels in which the herrings were salted and stored. Now there are hardly any herrings left.

Because we are away from port for such long periods – up to eight weeks if the fishing is poor – we have massive refrig-

Britain is a maritime nation but its fishing industry has suffered a severe decline over the last twenty years.

erators on board. The fish are frozen into blocks after gutting and stored below in the fish hold. On a good trip we may catch up to forty tons of fish a day. It fetches about £35–40 ($50–60) a kiss – that is 60 kg. (130 lb). So with a full load of fish on board, our catch is worth £250,000 ($375,000). About seventy per cent of that is spent just running the boat. After the skipper has taken his ten per cent of the remaining profit the rest is shared out amongst the men.

A good haul of fish waiting to be transported to the shops from the dockside market.

"Greed is the problem in this country"

Ray Anthony is 18. He lives with his parents in Birmingham, in the Midlands. He has been unemployed for much of the time since he left school but is currently engaged on a government work project.

I left school at 16 with no qualifications – I didn't like school. There were no jobs in Birmingham then, and things are even worse now. I went on the dole after about six weeks – one of more than three million unemployed in Britain.

Then I got the chance to go to college and learn a trade. It was a special college that took in kids that were unemployed. I did a one-year construction course. When we passed out with our diplomas we were supposed to get jobs as plumbers or bricklayers or carpenters. We were promised that local firms would come and take us on from the college. But only one of us out of twenty-five got a job, and that was as a postman!

So I had to go on the dole again. Luckily for me, two of my best mates were also on the dole. We went looking for work together: walking the streets and looking everywhere. After a while we got fed up with that and spent our time roller-skating around the Bullring shopping center in Birmingham. But we got bored with that in the end. We got bored with going to the Jobcenter in search of work too. It's supposed to be the place where they find you a job, but every time we went there we got the same answer, "You haven't got no qualifications and you haven't got no experience." It seemed that they just wanted to get rid of us.

Ray meets some of his friends in a café near the center of Birmingham.

Ray is lucky to be in a temporary job. Thousands of young people are currently unable to find work in Britain.

Now I'm working on a government youth opportunities scheme, getting experience as a dental technician – making false teeth and that sort of thing. The youth opportunities scheme was set up by the government a few years ago. It's supposed to give kids like us a chance to experience what it's like to have a full-time job with responsibilities. They send you to a company for six months' training. But you only get £25 a week to live on. This is paid to us by the employer and he claims it back from the government. We don't pay any tax or National Insurance and the employer gets cheap labor for six months. At the end of that, there's no guarantee of a full-time job. The employer just rings up the Jobcenter and they send around someone else. I think it's robbery.

Greed is the whole problem in this country. That's why there is so much unemployment. Everyone is pushing each other to the side so that they can make some quick money. Us kids are at the bottom of the pile.

At the moment I enjoy my job and I'd like to stay on after six months. But I'm not raising my hopes too high. I'll just wait and see. It's no use getting all excited just to be let down at the end of it. I still remember how wonderful we felt at that college when we were promised jobs then.

One of my mates got a job with a big company a few months ago. It seemed a secure position in the packing department and he saved up and bought a car. Then the company went bankrupt overnight and he was made redundant. Fancy being made redundant at 19. He's back on the dole now and has got to sell his car next week.

"People still like to see the written word"

Gill Swain is 31. She comes from Manchester but now works as a newspaper reporter on the *Daily Mail* newspaper which is based in Fleet Street in London.

The first daily newspaper in Britain was launched in 1702 but our most famous paper *The Times* did not appear until eighty-three years later. The *Daily Mail*, which is the paper I work for, was one of the first of the "popular" daily newspapers. Now there are five "popular" national dailies – the *Daily Mail*, the *Daily Express*, the *Sun*, the *Daily Mirror* and the *Daily Star* – and three "serious" daily newspapers – *The Times*, the *Guardian* and the *Daily Telegraph*.

Many of the nationals are based in London, where Fleet Street is the center of newspaper publishing. There are also about a hundred or so daily provincial papers published in cities and towns around the country and about 1,500 weeklies. All these newspapers are run by companies or by individuals and not by the government, although most papers do tend to support a particular political viewpoint.

Like most journalists, I began my career with a provincial paper – a weekly in Plymouth, Devon. From there I moved back to my home town of Manchester to work for the *Manchester Sunday People*. I started with the *Daily Mail* in 1979, initially as a summer relief reporter. It was supposed to last for only a few months, just filling in for reporters on holiday, but at the end of the summer they offered me a full-time post and I accepted, of course. The newspaper employs over 1,400 people: 350 of these are reporters, like me, editors or sub-editors.

It's a very different life here compared to the *Sunday People*. I don't feel so in touch with the readers on such a big newspaper. The main source of income for the nationals is from sales, whereas the weekly local papers rely mostly on advertisements to pay their production costs.

We print around three million copies a day of the *Daily Mail*. Like most other papers, it is printed at night. If you walk down Fleet Street at 3 a.m. it is buzzing with vans and men with great piles of

None of the hundred or so daily papers in Britain are run or owned by the state.

newspapers on their shoulders. They rush the morning editions to the mainline railway stations from where they are distributed to newsagents all over the country. From the newsagents they are delivered, often by young paper boys and girls, to over fifteen million homes every day.

Before the invention of TV and radio, it was the newspaper that broke the news of a major event to the public – few people knew what was going on in the world until they had read their morning paper. Things have changed now of course, but even with the advent of instant news media reports, video from overseas relayed by satellites and other sophisticated news-gathering devices, there is still a place for the newspaper. People like to see the written word and to read about things in greater detail than they can ever hope to get from the TV.

London's evening papers are often sold from newsstands like this one.

"Aberdeen is the 'oil capital' of Britain"

Andy Kay is 27. He comes from Oxford but spends two weeks of each month working as a roughneck on the Murchison oil production platform far out in the North Sea.

Oil was first discovered off the Scottish coast about twenty years ago, and Aberdeen has since become the "oil capital" of Britain. I've been involved in the industry for about four years. I went to university to study French and worked on a farm in France for a year. Although I enjoyed the life there, the money was awful. So one weekend I packed my bags and drove up to Aberdeen to see if the stories about big money in the oil industry were true.

Eventually I got a job on the Murchison Platform. It is owned by a consortium of international companies, including the British National Oil Corporation, and is operated by Conoco (U.K.) Ltd. The platform was the largest ever built in Britain when it was completed in 1979. It was floated out from Ardersier, near Inverness, on the mainland, and its four legs were positioned on the sea bed about 225 km. (140 miles) north-east of the Shetland Isles, in 200 m. (650 ft.) of water.

The platform cost millions of pounds to build and is very expensive to operate. It produces on average 80,000 barrels of oil a day (a barrel is about 200 liters or 52 gallons). The oil is pumped ashore to the Shetlands through a complicated system of pipelines linking up the thirty or so offshore platforms in this part of the North Sea. There are many other smaller exploratory rigs around the coast of Britain and oil has recently been discovered in Dorset.

I work on the drilling floor, 160 m. (520 ft.) above the sea, as a roughneck – the industry's name for a laborer. There are about thirty of us concerned with the drilling operation but there are upwards of 250 men on board the rig at any one time.

We drill down to 3,600 m. (11,800 ft.). There are twenty-four wellheads – that is, twenty-four holes radiating out from the platform. Each one takes about a month to drill. Once the wellheads are drilled we put down steel pipes, 10 m. (33 ft.) long. They are screwed together to extend all the way down to the oil-bearing sandstone.

The oil contains a great deal of natural

It's more a way of life than a job, working on a tiny platform like this far out in the North Sea. We work long hours, twelve a day, fourteen days at a time. But our living conditions are excellent. I share a room with four other men, but we are usually working different shifts so we rarely get in each other's way. The catering facilities are good too. There's always a fabulous choice of food and it's all provided free by the company. No alcohol of any kind is allowed on the platform – which is probably a good thing really. At the end of our two-week stint we get two weeks off and are flown back to the mainland by helicopter.

The routine is difficult for many of the workers' wives, especially those with young families. But it does mean that we get to spend six months of the year at home. There aren't that many jobs where you can do that!

Britain is now almost self-sufficient in oil from North Sea platforms like the Murchison.

Andy and other roughnecks watch as a critical stage is reached in the drilling of a new well.

gas when it reaches the platform. This gas is filtered off and burnt. Soon there will be a pipeline to pump it ashore like the oil but at the moment we have no storage facilities for such a vast quantity. It is said that we burn off enough gas each day on Murchison to satisfy the daily domestic requirements of a city the size of Edinburgh!

"Medical treatment is free in this country"

Beryl James is 31. She is a New Zealander who came to Britain on a working holiday and then decided to stay. Beryl now works for the National Health Service as a State Registered Nurse at Frimley Park Hospital, Surrey.

I left New Zealand nine years ago. Like so many Australians and New Zealanders I wanted to see historic Europe. New Zealand is such a young country by comparison. I only came to Britain on a working holiday but I'm still here! I worked for a while as an auxiliary nurse and enjoyed the hospital life so much that I decided to settle in England and take up nursing as a full-time career.

Most hospitals in Britain are run by the government under the control of the National Health Service (N.H.S.). Every working person in the country pays a National Insurance contribution and this, together with a proportion of the income tax we pay, goes towards the cost of running the service. So, although medical treatment is free in this country, it is paid for out of government funds.

The N.H.S. employs about one million people throughout Britain. Of these 450,000 are nurses; some are ambulance staff; there are engineers and architects; and, of course, thousands of doctors that have undertaken their six years' training.

Over twelve million pounds was spent in 1981 by the N.H.S. That is about five per cent of the total amount of money spent by central government.

The National Health Service provides free medical treatment for everyone living in Britain.

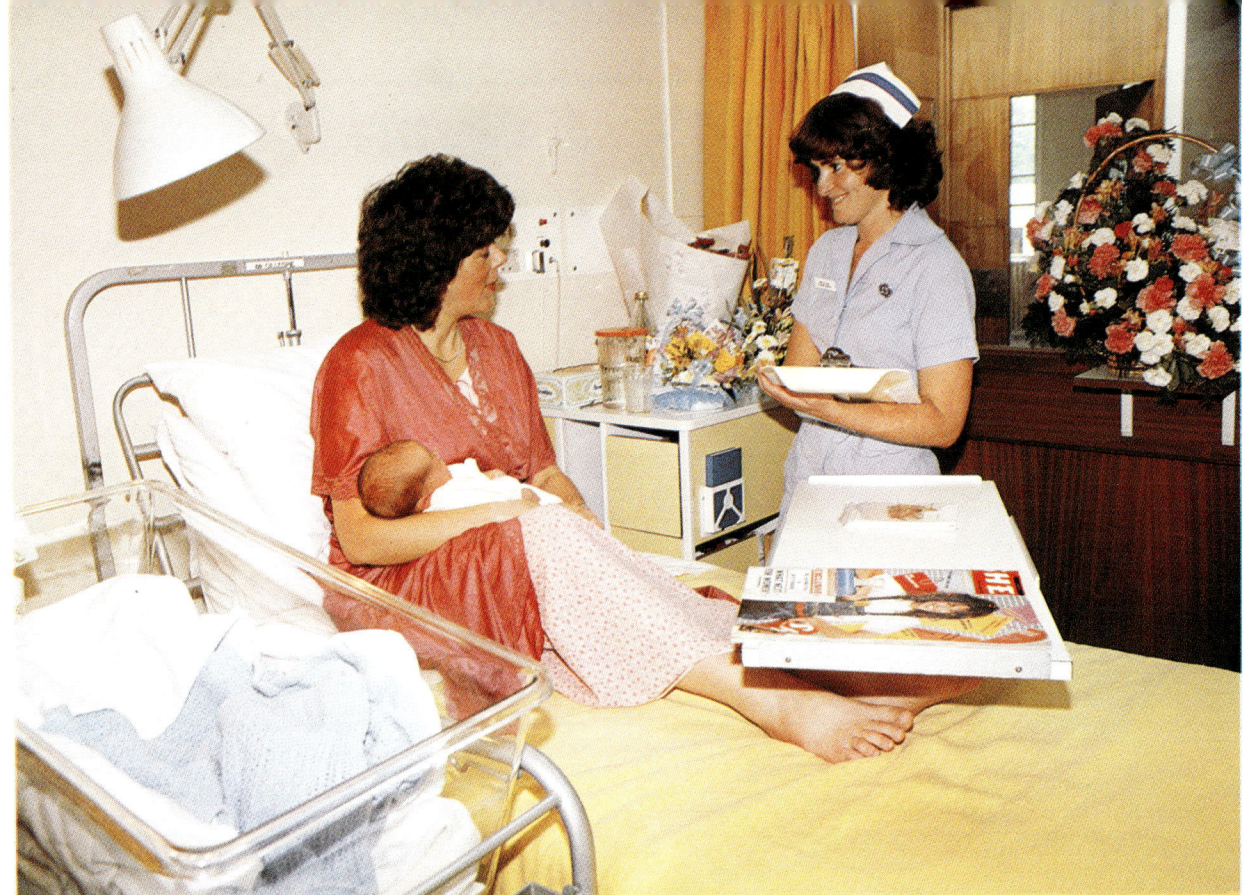

Student midwife Beryl chats to a mother soon after the delivery of her new baby.

Frimley Park is a typical British hospital. It was opened in 1974 and has 568 beds. It caters for the general needs of the community of West Surrey and East Hampshire. There are about 800 nurses and over a hundred doctors employed here.

There are two grades of nurses in this country – State Enrolled Nurses (S.E.N.s) and State Registered Nurses (S.R.N.s). To become one of either you have to take a course at a nursing school which is usually attached to a hospital. The S.E.N. course is two years long and the S.R.N. course is three years. I am a State Registered Nurse. When I first qualified, I worked as a staff nurse on one of the surgical wards at Frimley for just over a year, looking after men and women before and after their operations.

Now I am back in the classroom; this time learning midwifery. It is an interesting job in the maternity department, but like so many other jobs in the N.H.S. there is far too much paperwork. We really should have a receptionist on our ward; filling in forms is just not a job for an experienced and expensively trained nurse. But, like so many nationalized institutions in Britain, we have a shortage of funds and we all have to make do somehow.

In about a year's time I will sit my midwifery exams. If I pass as a fully qualified midwife I will be able to work as a staff midwife in a hospital or as a community midwife out "on the district" as we call it. Maybe by then, though, I will have decided to go back home to New Zealand or even to Australia to join the flying doctor service.

"We play for the enjoyment"

David Boorman is 33. He comes from Folkestone in Kent and once played cricket in the county league. He now works as a civil servant and lives in Horsham, Sussex. But he still plays cricket whenever he can.

It seems that some sort of game like cricket has been played for hundreds of years. But it was in the mid-eighteenth century that the British game really started. I doubt, though, whether they all wore white clothes like we do today, or even had eleven men to a side. All the local landowners had a team and they played each other at weekends. Men were hired and fired according to their ability to play the game. So that was the start of village cricket as we know it. The game soon spread to every corner of Britain.

Later the villages started to form local leagues and now there are often as many as twenty teams in such leagues who come from a radius of about 40 km. (24 miles). They make fixture lists (regular schedules) and play against each other on Saturdays or at holiday times.

It is every village cricketer's dream to play for his county. There are seventeen counties in Britain that field a professional side (team). The county teams are drawn from the best of the town and village teams. County teams now often play on Sundays in one-day play-off matches. They also play three-day matches, but this can lead to a slow game which few spectators find interesting enough to watch for that long.

There are also the international matches, or tests, of course. Seven teams in the world play under the governing body of the International Cricket Conference (I.C.C.). They are: Australia, the West Indies, New Zealand, India, Pakistan, Sri Lanka and England. They play each other on a rota basis. The first international match was played in the 1870s. In 1882 Australia first beat England; it was said that the British team was dead and that the Australians would take back the team's "ashes" with them. The following year the England team beat Australia in Melbourne. An Australian woman burnt the stumps, put them in a little urn and presented them to the English team. They are now kept at Lords, the famous English cricket ground in London, and every so often

A typical English village cricket match. Cricket is the national summer sport in Britain.

the two teams meet and play for the "Ashes."

I play for my local team at weekends. I should really love to play cricket every day of my life, but that is not possible! I'm just not good enough, I suppose, to be a professional. So every morning at 7:21, I catch the train from Horsham to London where I work in an office. Over 400,000 people commute from outside of London to their jobs in the capital.

I work as a civil servant in one of the many high-rise office blocks in the City of London. There are 666,400 civil servants in Britain. We are employed to administer and coordinate the many ministries and departments of central government. I work for the Ministry of Transport, which is responsible for all new road building in this country. It's an interesting job in a way, but I'd rather be strolling out onto newly mown grass with a bat over my shoulder.

The high-rise office blocks of the City of London where David works.

"We should be working for a better world"

Dr. Michael Dewar is 61. He is the rector of the Church of St John the Baptist in the parish of Helen's Bay, County Down, in Northern Ireland. He cannot understand why Catholics and Protestants should be fighting each other.

Most of the main religions are catered for in Northern Ireland, but the vast majority of people are either Roman Catholic or Protestant. The Church of Ireland used to be called the United Church of England and Ireland until it was disestablished in 1870. Like the Church of England it is Anglican but instead of being controlled by the Archbishop of Canterbury, it is controlled by the Bishop of Armagh.

I think that there is too much talk among Christians today of the difference between the separate churches that make up the faith. As Christians we all believe in the glory of one God and in His love for us all. We should all be working together in His name for a better world in which to live.

If you read the reports in the newspapers or watch the news on TV you would think that Northern Ireland is nothing but a seething mass of sectarian killings, with bombs going off on every street corner. Really, though, it's nothing like that. I live not more than 16 km. (10 miles) from the center of Belfast, the capital city and center of the troubles, but I could easily be in any quiet, sleepy corner of Britain.

I have been living at Helen's Bay now for ten years. It is a predominantly middle-class area with both Church of Ireland and Presbyterian congregations. Just 5 km. (3 miles) away is Bangor with a strong Catholic population. If you believe the newspapers we should be fighting in the streets, but instead we are holding fetes together; we work for Christian Aid Week together; and I am just starting a Boy Scout Troop that will have boys from every quarter.

Most of the people living here work on the land or in the offices of the capital. There is a lot of unemployment, of course. This has been caused not only by the unrest, but by the world recession in general. Especially hard hit has been the shipbuilding industry where competition from overseas is very fierce. In the past, many people left these shores to seek work in England. Now the situation is little

Dr. Dewar and his congregation outside St. John the Baptist Church in Helen's Bay.

better there and they are looking further afield to places like New Zealand and Canada. Toronto, I'm told, is like another Belfast.

The troubles in Northern Ireland do cast a shadow over our lives, but then we're used to trouble here. There's been fighting in Ireland for hundreds of years. Every so often something happens to make me wonder what the fighting is all about. Some years ago a Roman Catholic woman presented a beautiful stained-glass window to our church in memory of her mother, who was also a Catholic. The window depicts Saint Patrick, the patron saint of all Ireland. He casts his light upon us all – Catholics and Protestants. This present from a Roman Catholic to a Protestant church is indicative of the good faith that still exists in Northern Ireland, despite the last fourteen years of the bomb and the bullet.

Despite fourteen years of violence, life in Belfast goes on quite normally.

"I just about get by on my grant"

Jenny Smith is 22. She comes from Cambridge, but at present is studying classics at Exeter College, Oxford University, where she is in the third year of a four-year course.

People are often surprised that I came to Oxford to attend university when I grew up in Cambridge, Britain's other famous university city. The reason is that not all the forty-three universities in Britain offer the same courses. I wanted to study classics (Latin and Greek literature and history) and there are only about three places in the country where I can take that course.

Oxford and Cambridge universities have a reputation for being the best in Britain. This may have been the case in the past but there are a lot of people who would argue with that now! Certainly, though, they are amongst the largest. Oxford has over 15,000 students at its twenty-three colleges. There are 9,000 undergraduates (those who have yet to take their final exams) and 6,000 post-graduates (those who stay on after their finals and continue to do research). Exeter College has 280 undergraduates and ninety post-grads, so we are quite a small college.

When I first came I lived in a hall of residence (dormitory). Most universities find quarters for students in their first year. I was lucky enough to be able to stay in halls for my second year as well. However, I'm now in my third year so I've had to find my own accommodation. In a university city like Oxford, this can be a real problem. I share a house on the

Jenny with her bicycle in the city center in Oxford.

58

outskirts of town with some other students and we share the rent and other expenses between us.

I get a grant from my local education authority in Cambridge to help me study. It is supposed to be enough to pay my rent, clothe me, feed me and entertain me for eight months of the year. My parents pay part of the grant because they can afford to, but some students' parents are quite hard up and cannot afford to pay much towards the total, even though they are supposed to. It's a very unfair system: some parents really cannot afford to pay their share and this makes it really hard on the student. I just about get by on my grant, but it doesn't amount to very much.

I have to do a lot of reading for my course – over one hundred books a year. Each week I have to write one or two essays. But life at university is not all academic study. There are many clubs and societies. I'm a member of the Oxford Union Debating Scoiety. We have regular guest speakers and it's a place to meet friends and relax. There are also cinema and theater clubs as well as excellent sports facilities.

Because Oxford is on the River Thames we have a reputation for rowing. I'm a cox, the person who steers and controls the boat. There are eight men plus the cox in each boat. We take part in races throughout the year both against other Oxford colleges and against other universities. Every year Oxford fields a team against our greatest rivals – Cambridge. It is the highlight of the rowing calendar in Britain and attracts many thousands of spectators who line the banks of the Thames in London to watch the contest. Last year Oxford won with a girl cox, so maybe there is hope for me yet!

With Jenny, the cox, at the stern one of the crews at Oxford sets off for a practice row on the River Thames.

"The fourth largest company in the world"

Dayle Hunt is 21. He lives in Sevenoaks in Kent and travels to the other side of the Thames Estuary to Dagenham in Essex every day to work at the giant Ford Motor Company assembly plant.

I'm a relief worker on the production line at Ford. The cars move slowly along on conveyors and we have to walk along as we work on them. Over the past three years I've learned all the different jobs that have to be done in our department, which is concerned with making sure that the lighting components are fixed and working properly and with putting in some of the trim to the door panels and roof.

Ford is the fourth largest company in the world. Some of its cars, such as the Granada, Capri and some Fiestas are made on the Continent in Spain, Belgium and Germany. Ford (U.K.) Ltd. produce 350,000 cars a year in Britain. They employ over 70,000 workers at twenty-four locations, although Dagenham is the largest. Here we see about 800 a day pass along the production line. That's a lot of money at an average of £4,000 ($6,000) each. Two models are made here: the Fiesta and the Cortina.

Nearly everyone at Dagenham belongs to a trade union. I belong to the Transport and General Workers' Union (T.G.W.U.) but most of the major unions are represented here. Each section of the shop floor has a union shop steward. Although he is employed by Ford, his main job is to see that the work-force is being looked after properly by the company. Any problems relating to working conditions or pay are reported to him and he in turn liaises with the convenor who goes to the management. The relationship between workers and management at Ford is excellent and this is due mostly to the understanding of the problems of car production by both the unions and the management. You hear a lot about strikes in the car industry in Britain, but we have very few at Ford.

There is a great deal of foreign competition in the British car market. Recently, there has been a massive increase in the number of good, cheap cars coming from Japan and from other European countries. Our main competitor, though, is the nationalized company, British Leyland (B.L.). We at Ford are proud of the fact that despite all competition we still have the largest share of the market.

The company spends millions of pounds every year on research and development. The modern motorist wants a car that is well-styled but reasonably priced; small but comfortable; and fast and economical enough to tackle the many kilometers of motorway that have been built in Britain since the early sixties.

Many drivers take their cars to the Continent where the roads don't have the 112 k.p.h. (70 m.p.h.) speed limits that we have in this country, so they need a safe and reliable car capable of much higher speeds than in the past. Many manufacturers can supply such a car, but we think Ford does it better. That is why everyone here drives one!

Nearly all cars in Britain are made on mass-production assembly lines like this one.

Many hundreds of kilometers of highway have been built in Britain since the 1960s.

Facts

Britain comprises England, Scotland and Wales. Together with Northern Ireland it forms the United Kingdom of Great Britain. England is divided geographically into 45 counties, Wales into 8 counties, Northern Ireland into 6 counties and Scotland into 9 regions.

Capital city: London.

Languages: The official language is English but Welsh is widely spoken in Wales.

Race: Britain has, as a yearly average, more emigrants than immigrants. In the past, there were major influxes in the 1930s (of refugees from Europe) and in the 1960s (of people from Commonwealth countries).

Currency: 100 pence (p) = one pound sterling (£1) or about U.S. $1.50.

Religion: In England, and Wales, the Church of England is the established church. The Church of England baptizes forty per cent of babies born in England. The Church of Scotland is the established church there. In Northern Ireland there are about 480,000 Roman Catholics, 405,000 Presbyterians, and 335,000 members of the Church of Ireland and Church of England.

Population: The population of England, Scotland and Wales was, according to a 1982 estimate, 55,700,000. The Netherlands is the only other major European country more overcrowded than England and Wales. The population of Northern Ireland in 1978 was estimated at 1,538,000.

Climate: Generally cool temperate, but variable.

Government: Britain is a constitutional monarchy with a sovereign as the head of state. Parliament comprises two houses. The House of Commons has 650 members elected for a maximum of five years by direct suffrage. The House of Lords comprises hereditary peers (nobles) of the realm and life peers and peeresses created by a sovereign. Executive power is vested in the Cabinet, headed by the Prime Minister.

The Secretary of State for Northern Ireland is answerable to Parliament for the government of Northern Ireland. Northern Ireland sends members to the United Kingdom Parliament.

Local administration in Britain is carried out by many different bodies including:

Local branches of some central government institutions (for example, the Department of Health and Social Security and the Department of Employment).

Local departments of nationalized industries (for example, the post office and public transport).

Specialist authorities (for example, water).

Local government at three levels – county councils, district councils and parish councils (Welsh community council). England also has some metropolitan county and district councils. Northern Ireland has a single level system of twenty-six district councils.

Housing: There are four times more houses than apartments in Britain and more dwellings available than families. Nevertheless, there are housing shortages. More than two in five families live in a post-1945 home, and over half of all dwellings are owner-occupied. One-third is rented from public housing authorities and the remainder is rented from private landlords.

Education: Schooling is compulsory from ages 5–16 and there are two systems: one publicly maintained by local education authorities (L.E.A.s) and free; one privately maintained and fee-paying. The education system is structured as follows:

Up to age 5 children can attend one of 663 nursery schools, which are mostly part-time. From ages 5–11 children attend primary schools, although there exist some middle schools taking children from age 9–13.

At secondary level 11–16 (or 18) there are some selective schools (called grammar schools), although most secondary schools are now comprehensive and non-selective.

There are 650 institutions of higher education and 43 universities.

In Northern Ireland a similar system exists. Fees are paid in preparatory schools but most schools are maintained by L.E.A.s. There are two universities.

Agriculture: Mainly comprising livestock farming, agriculture employs 2.6 per cent of the total working population. The main crops are: cereals, fodder crops, sugar, potatoes, hops, fruit, vegetables and flowers.

Industry: Britain is one of the world's major industrial and exporting countries with 29 per cent of its working population engaged in manufacturing (35 per cent in Northern Ireland). Most manufacturing is carried out by private enterprises although there are some nationalized industries. Main industries are: engineering, electrical goods, and textiles. Petroleum and coal deposits have recently been found in the North Sea. The economy is depressed with unemployment around 3 million.

Media: Britain has the world's third highest newspaper circulation per head of population. There are 124 daily and Sunday newspapers. No paper is owned directly by a political party.

Television broadcasting is under the control of the British Broadcasting Corporation (B.B.C.) and the Independent Broadcasting Authority (I.B.A.). The B.B.C. controls two TV channels: B.B.C.1 and B.B.C.2; 4 national radio channels; and many local radio stations. It is financed through license fees. The I.B.A. controls 14 independent regional TV channels served by 15 TV program companies. It is financed by the sale of advertising time. There are many independent radio stations.

The government has no general access to radio or TV.

Glossary

alluvial Deposited by rivers and streams, or by flood.
anthracite A type of hard coal that burns with little smoke or flame.
barrister A lawyer or counsel who manages cases for clients in court.
colliery A coal mine and its buildings.
comprehensive school A school accommodating children of all abilities.
constituency The area of the country, or the voters within that area, who are represented in Parliament by an M.P.
crofter A person who subsistence farms a small area of land.
disestablished Deprived of established status.
dole The payment given by the state to unemployed people.
fen Low-lying, marshy ground.
grammar school In the recent past, a British school for academically proficient children.
heifer A cow too young to give milk.
liquefied gas Gas that is made into a liquid under pressure.
maroon An exploding flare used as a signal.
midwife A woman who assists women in childbirth.
M.P. Member of Parliament.
nationalized Made the property of the state.
new town A town created especially to supply relief housing and employment.
orienteering Cross-country hiking, guided only by a compass and surveyor's map.
petrol *Brit* Gasoline.
potholing The hobby of exploring caves; spelunking.
publican *Chiefly Brit* The licensee of a public house (pub).
public school The British equivalent of a private school in the U.S.
scree A heap or slope of stones or rocky debris.
sectarian Belonging or relating to sects, or religious groups.
selective school A school accepting academically proficient children.
stumps Posts; parts of the wickets used in the game of cricket.

Index

agriculture 62
    dairy farming 8–9
    and the E.E.C. 30–1
    market gardening 30–1

beer 22–3
Belfast 18–19, 56–7

canals 38
car industry 7, 61–2
Church of Ireland 56–7
City of London 34, 55
civil service 42, 45
climate 19, 25, 33, 62
coal mining 6–7
Conservative Party 42
crime 13

dairy farming 8–9
Daily Mail 48
Dartmoor National Park 23
drama 28–9

Edinburgh 32–3
education 20–1, 36–7, 58–9, 62
E.E.C., The
    and agriculture 30–1
    and food prices 27
    and politics 42
elections 42
Elizabeth II, Queen 42
energy 6–7, 21, 50–1
English Channel 27
European Parliament 42
exports 15, 19

ferry services 26–7
fishing industry 11, 44–5
Fleet Street 48
flora and fauna 15, 19
folk singing 40–1
food 23, 39
    Moslem 17
Ford (U.K.) Ltd. 61–2

Government, system of 42–3, 62
    and the Arts 29
    and education 37, 59
    and the media 48, 49
    and medical treatment 52–3
    and unemployment 47

Grampian Highlands 15
Greater London Council 35

Highland Games 32
Hogmanay 38
hospitals 52–3
housing 7, 58–9, 62

immigrants 16–17, 62
industry 61–2
    car production 7,
    coal mining 6–7
    fishing 11, 44–5
    oil 50–1
    shipbuilding 18–19, 56
    whiskey distilling 14–15
Isle of Skye 24–5

language 21, 62
Labour Party 42
law and order 12–13
Liberal Party 42
local government 62
    and education 37, 59, 62
    and transport 34–5
Loch Ness 38–9
Loch Ness Monster 32, 39

market gardening 30–1
media 48–9, 63
medical treatment 52–3
Morris dancing 40

National Coal Board 6
National Health Service 52–3
national parks 20, 23
natural gas 51
New Covent Garden market 31
new towns 13

oil industry 50–1

Palace of Holyroodhouse 33
police force 10–11
politics 42–3
population 62
postal service 24
public houses (pubs) 22–3
public transportation 24–5

racial problems 16

religion
    Anglican 56, 57
    Moslem 16, 17
    Roman Catholic 37, 56, 57
retailing 16–17
Royal National Lifeboat
    Institution 10–11
Royal Shakespeare
    Company 28–9

Shakespeare, William 28–9
shipbuilding industry 18–19, 56
Snowdonia National Park 20
Social Democratic Party 42
sports
    cricket 54–5
    fishing 15, 38
    Highland Games 32
    mountaineering 20–1
    rowing 59
    rugby 7
    shooting 15

trade unions 61
tourism 21, 38–9

Underground, The 34
unemployment 46–7
universities 58–9

whiskey distilling industry 14–15
wildlife 15

Youth Opportunities Scheme 47

WITHDRAWN

AAA-5016